I0149644

All Scripture references taken from the KJV of the Holy Bible, unless otherwise indicated.

In Multiplying, I Will Multiply Thee

by Dr. Marlene Miles

Freshwater Press 2024

freshwaterpress9@gmail.com

ISBN: 978-1-963164-74-9

Paperback Version

Table of Contents

In Multiplying
I Will Multiply
Thee

Freshwater Press, USA

Be

God breathed into man, and he became a living soul. Now man exists. Now he *is*. Now, he *be*.

In Him we move and breathe and have *being*.

For in him we live, and move, and have our being; as certain also of your own poets have said, For we are also his offspring. (Acts 17:28)

In Him we live. Without the Lord we can do nothing. Without the Lord we would not *be*. Without the Lord, we would have no being. We would remain inanimate clay objects if we were even formed, without the breath of God, without the *Zoe*, the Life of God within us. So, with this Life we now can be spoken to with understanding. We can hear. We can be taught, instructed, directed, given assignments and purpose.

Abide in me, and I in you. As the branch cannot bear fruit of itself, except it abide in the vine; no more can ye, except ye abide in me. I am the vine, ye *are* the branches: He that abideth in me, and I in him, the same bringeth forth much fruit: for without me ye can do nothing. (John 15:4-5)

Before you can do anything, you must first be. You must be chosen of God to have breath, to have life. You must receive and use the breath and know that it is on loan from God. However, spiritual beings that do not have bodies cannot *do* because they have no bodies, therefore we must have both things in tandem and working in conjunction one with another to accomplish what we were sent here to accomplish.

Without knowing that we are multitaskers, we must be multitaskers who *live, breathe, **be**,* and *do.*

Hear & Do

God said in Genesis to creation and to the animals He had created: *Be fruitful and multiply.*

That Word also applies to Adam whom He had given both life and a wife: *Be fruitful and multiply.*

When God spoke, **Be fruitful and multiply** all of creation heard it.

The voice of the Lord is upon many waters; the voice of the Lord thunders. You can be in a prophetic service, for example, and hear a Word given to someone, but you know that Word is also for you. No matter how the speaker speaks, when they are giving voice to the words that are coming from God, it sounds different, it sounds amplified, it sounds important, and grabs your attention. It can be as though those words are **thundering**.

- It could be for you because God rains on the just and the unjust alike.
- It could be for you because dogs eat crumbs from the master's table. I'm calling no one a dog, but a person might not even be saved and in that service.
- Or, maybe you are saved and you're in that sanctuary. That Word could be for you because God is the God of More Than Enough and even the overflow of God is substantial. The glory of God as He passes by is so great that a man could die from just seeing all that glory.

You also can be in a regular church service and what a preacher says is only what he is saying, when he is speaking out of his own flesh. But when the preacher speaks as the oracles, or as the mouthpiece of God, when a man or a woman speaks a certain way and speaks a *certain* Word, you and so many, if not all in the congregation, with **ears** to hear know that the Word is also for them. That Word is for each one of them and they hear it in the way that the Lord has designed and ordained them to hear that Word.

God said in Deuteronomy 4:10, ***Gather me the people together, and I will speak to them.***

In the same way you make statements or proclamations or set rules in your own home you do it in earshot of all so that the entire family knows that this rule is for us. This word is for us. This blessing is for us. This command and this commandment are for us.

In the Book of Exodus when Moses went up on Mount Sinai, he went to get the Word of God for the people. The people were restless and foolish, and newly freed, and behaving like wild, unmannered children or teenagers who just got out of their parents' house on their own for the first time. Those at the foot of the mountain decided to not wait on that prophet, Moses, and to not wait on the Word, but did their own thing in the time that Moses was up on the mountain.

Still, they are responsible to do the Word that the prophet came down and gave to them, whether they were attentive or not. They still are responsible to **do** the Word the prophet gave whether they liked those words or not. They are still responsible to do the Word given by God whether their own ears were listening, or whether they were there or not or even if it was told to them by hearsay. None of us reading this book were there physically, but because a *representative* from our bloodline was there and these are generational commandments we are still responsible to do what the Lord spoke because what He spoke were commandments.

They were commandments, not good ideas, life hacks, or suggestions.

When God said to creation and Adam and Eve, **Be fruitful and multiply**, that Word was for all of us too, and even now because God had gathered ALL the people together when He spoke those words. At that time Adam and Eve were *all* the people. All the people were in Adam & Eve, prophetically.

Do not forsake the assembling of yourself together because in the assembly, God will speak and He will say things that you are responsible to know, to be, and to do.

God can speak to many of us at once; God can speak to all of us at once, if He so desires. And we are expected to have heard the same thing.

Listen

Be fruitful and multiply.

God assembled the people, *His* people in the Garden of Eden. As was His custom, in the cool of the day He came down and walked with them. They were assembled; He spoke, they both listened. When all the people are together, they can hear the same thing at the same time and there can be no dissension regarding what was said.

I know a businessman who is famous for telling his staff, *Don't make me repeat myself.* God is far more gracious than that, but if He says what He says once, then He doesn't waste time repeating Himself, as well.

Unless He has to. Unless it is critically important. Unless man is not listening. Man can be hardheaded and hard of hearing, or not have *ears to hear*.

From Mount Sinai, Moses broke the first tablets written by the Finger of God, then Moses had to chisel another set. As far as I am concerned, that is God having to repeat Himself. This is not what God meant by multiplying things. God was Merciful and repeated the Commandments a third time, to all the people, but this time through a cloud. He is gracious to give us the Law, even though He had to repeat Himself. We need the Law; it is for our protection.

God spoke to all those people at once; therefore, they were expected to have understood what He said and understood the same thing in the same way.

Take a moment to recall that when the Serpent came into the Garden he came to Eve, not to Adam and Eve at the same time. And he is still using that tactic of divide and conquer. He is still telling folks different things, and if those folks don't communicate, they will never know if they've been lied to or not.

Little girls and females are more likely to tell everything, sometimes more than they should; perhaps we've learned our lesson. The old folks say, *Tell the truth, shame the devil.*

Males on the other hand are often quieter and less likely to spill beans that don't need to be spilled. Sometimes it is like pulling teeth to get a guy to tell you things that he may think are not important. As long as the devil is able to tell folks in a family, or in a marriage, or a workplace, or a church different things, different versions of the same story, or straight up lies on one another, if we don't communicate with one another, the devil can run all over that place.

Tell the truth; once the devil is exposed, he is defeated. He hides in the dark and in secrecy.

Creation Obeys

In Genesis when God said, ***Be fruitful and multiply***, not only did **all** the people--, both Adam AND Eve hear it, but also all of creation heard it. All of Creation includes plants, animals and every living thing that God created.

Creation is smarter than man, although man doesn't think so. Creation obeys its Creator, absent evil interference.

Man? Well not always, even though he should obey God, he is responsible to and he must be accountable when he does not. Nothing resists God except foolish, ignorant, and rebellious man. The only way Creation would ever disobey God is when it is told to disobey God, when it is escorted by man, who has authority in the Earth and when that man, himself decides to listen to flesh, demons, or the devil himself and then he commands, tricks, and/or escorts Creation into disobedience.

Abram & Sarai

Abram married Sarai in Genesis Chapter 11.

Now will I sing to my wellbeloved a
song of my beloved touching his
vineyard. My wellbeloved hath a
vineyard in a very fruitful hill:
(Isaiah 5:1 NAS)

Getting married is the beginning of being fruitful and multiplying. Getting married signifies that you are now planning to be fruitful and multiply. When men looked for spouses back in the times of the Bible, they were supposedly looking for those who could bear them children, especially. Women were pleased to find men that were providers. He was looking for a vineyard, and she was looking for a fruitful hill, or vice versa. Well, you can make what you will of the above verse, but to me it is all about bearing children.

Even though Abram was still Abram and not yet Abraham, he still was under the *Be Fruitful and Multiply* mandate since it applied to all of Creation. Abram was from Ur and those people there were astrologers--, talk about New Age, there is no such thing, it is Old Age, pagan stuff—repackaged, over and over.

So, Abram and Sarai take a trip down to Egypt and Abram, for the first time, because he will do it again, tells Sarai to tell the king that she is his sister. Well, that's half true because Sarai was the half-sister to Abram – eww! IKR. Anyway, Sarai obeys her husband and King Abimelech takes her into the palace and God didn't like that, therefore God shut up the wombs of all the women in the palace; everyone became barren suddenly. God turned **off** multiplication because of sin. That sin was Sarai, a married woman, being in the palace with the King.

Fortunately, nothing happened between the King and Sarai. God gave the king a dream and told him the 4-1-1 on Sarai, so he let her go. God then again opened up the wombs of all the ladies in the palace so they could get pregnant and bear children.

Be Fruitful and Multiply is a commandment of God, it is an authority of God, it is a permission of God that He gives to man. But we also see God can suspend it, He can flip that switch and turn it off if He doesn't want something copied or replicated, promoted, or ***multiplied***.

By the same token, since God can do that, He can enhance multiplication as well. That's what He was going to do for Abraham—multiply his seed, giving him numerous offspring, as many as the sands in the seashore, as plenteous as the stars…

Thou shalt be blessed above all people: there shall not be male or female barren among you, or among your cattle. (Deuteronomy 7:14)

This is God blessing the Israelites as they were coming out of Egypt.

Glory to God.

God is so serious about this. The married people will be having children, and their livelihoods will prosper – at that time it was cattle and farming and whatnot so even the cattle would be multiplying.

We saw that with Abraham's grandson, Jacob, whose cattle increased significantly when he was with Laban. Jacob was with Laban who was not his friend. A non-friend is an enemy. Laban was planning to keep ripping Jacob off, but GOD had blessed Jacob in Abraham. God had renewed the covenant in Isaac, his dad, and even though Jacob stole the blessing of the firstborn, his twin brother, Esau, he still had it and was being blessed and multiplied by GOD because Jacob was obedient to what he had agreed to with Laban even though Laban was being dishonest.

The New Testament states that God will avenge all disobedience in your obedience.

You do what you're supposed to do: God's got it. Do not seek vengeance.

Do you realize that if you send a curse to someone who actually prays and they just say one random *back to sender* to you, you just cursed yourself? If it doesn't hit you, do you realize it will find your generations? Do you not realize that it will find your children and your *children's* children? The sender-backer may not even know what they are sending back, but if they say it, the arrow must obey it.

So far, I have not found a prayer or verbiage to send back and arrow that was sent back to the original sender. The only way to do that is with another curse and another curse, or a curse from a higher, more wicked altar. Regarding cursing people and attending wicked altars, we should not have anything to do with that kind of stuff. We do not want to participate in or escalate any evil.

Leave vengeance to God.

Abrahamic Covenant

That in blessing I will bless thee, and in multiplying I will multiply thy seed as the stars of the heaven, and as the sand which is upon the sea shore; and thy seed shall possess the gate of his enemies; (Genesis 22:17)

And I will make thy seed to multiply as the stars of heaven, and will give unto thy seed all these countries; and in thy seed shall all the nations of the earth be blessed; (Genesis 26:4)

At first it may seem odd that if **Be Fruitful and Multiply** is already working in the Earth why does God have to tell Abraham all the particulars that He shared with him in making covenant with Abraham. But Abraham didn't start out as saved, he was a pagan, so God was getting him up to speed on how great it is to be in the Kingdom of God and what the benefits are. Not only that, but God was also bringing Abraham up to speed, quickly and mightily.

We are in Abraham, so it would behoove us to know what is in the Abrahamic Covenant, as well. Know it. Believe it. Stand on it. Receive the blessings of it from the Lord.

Isaac & Jacob

The Abrahamic Covenant was generational, therefore God renewed it with Abraham's son, Isaac.

Isaac redug the wells that Abraham had dug. In those days a man with a well was independent and either wealthy or on his way to being wealthy. People and animals need water. Do you recall that when Abraham sent his servant to get a wife for Isaac, that Rebekkah helped the man get water for himself and also for his camels? Being offered water in those days, in that area, in that climate especially was life.

Owning a well was the sign of a man who was blessed, and blessed by God. Wells weren't left or abandoned, they were handed down as generational wealth. Having a well indicated that you were allowed to live in that land, or that you were supposed to be there. Every time Isaac dug, he wasn't digging for gold or diamonds, he was digging for life—for his own livelihood and that of his family and his cattle and crops. We should be so diligent to dig into and search out the Word of God for in it is Life. In it is the blessing of God; in it is favor and the favor of God is Life.

Jesus took this to a whole new level when He asked the Samaritan woman for water at the well. That whole lesson is a marvel to me and it typifies what Jesus' ministry was about. He asked the woman for plain old water, a cup to drink, perhaps and in exchange He could and would give her Living Water so that she would never thirst again. Jesus' ministry is all about the great exchange.

God's Covenant with Abraham's bloodline was renewed again with Isaac's son, Jacob as it was to be passed down to their generations. Folks, that includes us that are in Christ right now. Amen.

I include many verses in this volume for **emphasis** to let you see how many times God reiterated the Covenant and reaffirmed it to show how important this was for God, for the plan of mankind, for the plan of Redemption and for the generations of Abraham to get this into their heads. God talks about multiplying His people at least 52 times over 17 verses, so it must be very important to Him and to mankind. It is a serious blessing.

That's us, folks; read it. Hear it. Listen: *we* are the generations of Abraham. We are as numerous as the stars in the sky, we are too many to count as the sand on the seashore. We are the righteousness of God, in Christ Jesus because Christ was in Abraham, and we know we are in Christ.

Be it. Do it. Live it.

And the LORD appeared unto him the
same night, and said, I am the God of
Abraham thy father: fear not, for I am
with thee, and will bless thee,
and multiply thy seed for my servant
Abraham's sake. (Genesis 26:24)

And God Almighty bless thee, and
make thee fruitful, and multiply thee,
that thou mayest be a multitude of
people; (Genesis 28:3)

And said unto me, Behold, I will make
thee fruitful, and multiply thee, and I
will make of thee a multitude of
people; and will give this land to thy
seed after thee for an everlasting
possession. (Genesis 48:4)

And he removed from thence, and
digged another well; and for that they
strove not: and he called the name of it
Rehoboth; and he said, For now
the LORD hath made room for us, and
we shall be fruitful in the land.
(Genesis 26:22)

And God said unto him, I am God
Almighty: be fruitful and multiply; a
nation and a company of nations
shall be of thee, and kings shall come
out of thy loins; (Genesis 35:11)

In Blessing

Who doesn't want to be blessed? Everyone wants to be blessed, feel blessed, look blessed. We want others to know we are blessed. We all like to say, *I'm blessed and highly favored in the Name of Jesus.*

Lord, make me a blessing.

LORD, bless me to be a blessing in the Name of Jesus.

God made covenant with Abraham in Chapter 17 saying that He would bless Abraham, give him all that land, as far as his eye could see, multiply him with descendants, there would be so many of them, stars in the sky, sands on the shore would not be able to compete for number. God said He would multiply Abraham with descendants, and there would be Redemption.

That in blessing I will bless thee, and in multiplying I will multiply thy seed as the stars of the heaven, and as the sand which is upon the sea shore; and thy seed shall possess the gate of his enemies;

And in thy seed shall all the nations of the earth be blessed; because thou hast obeyed my voice.
(Genesis 22:17-18)

In blessing, I will bless thee.

Except for the greediest and most selfish, most of us have that *in blessing* part of this Scripture figured out very well. We hear it from the pulpit every week, sometimes multiple times in a week. The pastor not only says, *It is more blessed to give than it is to receive,* he also finds things for us to give to, the Missionaries, or the Building Fund.

Sometimes he tells us what to give and when to give and to whom we should give.

I'm often confused and disappointed that the church doesn't have enough money to do what they want to do. It is unsettling, it leads to feelings of uncertainty and insecurity; it is stressful. It counters faith because we serve a God who is more than enough.

Do we not have enough because the church is trying to do what they want to do instead of what God said do? If we stay within the parameters of what God said He would totally provide.

Has God forgotten to send provision for the Vision? I don't think so. Therefore, what is the problem? Is it the vision? I doubt it.

Is it the people in the building? Is it us? Is it the congregants? Is it the leadership? We can only know that if we ask God. One sinner can destroy much good because one sinner is like a household witch and can open the door for evil to come right into that congregation and sit amongst the saints, even in the pews.

I've been in churches where there is a surprise giving moment. I've never understood this one, but it's someone's birthday and for some reason we are supposed to bring money up to them and give it or even hand it to them.

I don't know this person, and we don't give for everyone's birthday, so this escapes my understanding. It REALLY escapes my understanding because we don't even celebrate birthdays in that church. Well, we are taught that birthdays are spiritually precarious times, and it is best to fast and pray on one's birthday rather than live it up. When I Googled that, and you know I did, we see that Christians never used to celebrate birthdays, that was a pagan tradition, so I suppose giving money to a guy because he got a year older is not pagan because the pastor said that we are now blessed to give?

Of a truth, the pastor should know the season for giving. We expect that he is hearing from God and when he says give, the spiritual land should be fertile, and our seeds should prosper now and in that field. However, when looking for biblical precedent I only found, *Rejoice with those who rejoice* and *Your gift will make room for you*, that is if you are going to see a king or other dignitary or person of honor, you bring an appropriate gift. And, we should also give to the poor and the less fortunate.

A birthday card? A birthday gift? Thank you, Hallmark. This is a manmade construct.

The Word says that he who gives his wealth to the rich, I paraphrase, that man is a fool.

and he that giveth to the
rich, *shall* surely *come* to want.
(Proverbs 22:16B)

One of the most moving moments I have ever seen or experienced in a church was on a Wednesday night Bible Study. After the teaching portion, the pastor compassionately said, "*Anyone in here who is facing a deadline this week and you do not know how you are going to make it, come up to this altar.*"

My God of Mercy! That's an altar call that will take courage and humility for anyone to truthfully walk up there.

Without having to be asked a second time, a few people got out of their seat, and they came up.

Everyone who had an upcoming issue came up and faced him, probably expecting prayers from the pulpit.

But then he said, "*Turn around and face the congregation.*"

And they did.

He then said, *"Saints of God,"* speaking to the congregation, *"this is your chance to do one another ministry."*

All the people in the place were about to burst into tears--, everyone. While we are turning to our neighbor and fake hugging them, which you know is my pet peeve, we don't know how they are suffering. While we are turning to our pew neighbor and saying, *Get ready, get ready, get ready*, we don't know that they don't have anything to get ready **with**. They also may not have enough faith to even try to get ready for anything. This is why I say we should look people in the eye when we see them and talk to them, so we can know how they are really doing.

On that Wednesday night, people got out of their seats and came up to the front where those in need were standing and pressed whatever the Lord put on their hearts into the hands of those standing, broken, and humbled at that altar.

That is proper almsgiving, that was a move of the Spirit; that was the LORD.

Jesus said, ***The poor you have with you always.*** We should endeavor to bring one another up, we should invite people and help people to level up, in the Name of Jesus. I'm sure those who received were blessed, but I'm also sure that those who gave were as blessed, or MORE blessed as the Scripture states. Because it is more blessed to give than it is to receive. Of a truth, usually the ***more blessed*** are the ones giving, versus the ones receiving.

We are trained as kids and from childhood that it is more blessed to give than to receive. Yet, receiving is a blessing, else the Word would not have said, *The blessings of the Lord maketh rich and he addeth no sorrow with it.* That lets me know that every "blessing" does not make rich, and neither does every "blessing" bring joy and or peace, instead some can bring sorrow.

There is only one place where the words *more* and *blessed* are put together in that juxtaposition:

I have shewed you all things, how that so labouring ye ought to support the weak, and to remember the words of the Lord Jesus, how he said, It is more blessed to give than to receive.
(Acts 20:35)

The condition of a blessed man describes the man, and it describes what happens to a man who receives. That man is made happy, he is pronounced happy. Every time I have ever given, I am blessed *for* giving, *in* giving, and for having enough to share in the first place. I am *more blessed.*

Spiritual happiness means a man has found the favor of God and the joys of being in the Kingdom of Heaven. God takes pleasure in the prosperity of His servants. The joy of the Lord is my strength. When we are blessed, we are fortunate, and we feel fortunate.

When We Don't Give

The distortion of this is when folks actively look for others who are less fortunate than themselves so they can feel good about themselves. This is a perversion of what God intended, and it is ungodly. If we seek out the conditions of others and find them needy or lacking, then we give, as the Word says.

There are times, however, when we should not give. Therefore, we must be discerning: we don't give by unsanctioned Mercy--, did God say give? We don't give to everyone we see, or everyone who asks, and we don't give them everything that they ask for.

I confused a man once when I asked him if everything his daughter asks for, she gets? I asked him, *"Is the answer to every question, yes?"* What I asked him had never occurred to him. He was like a puppet or a robot, when his daughter spoke, he jumped into action. Yet, this is how spoiled brats are made.

The answers to our prayers are yes and amen, but God doesn't make spoiled brats. There are requirements

We don't give to the kingdom of darkness. We don't give to those who are trying to kill us or take us down. We don't give to those under judgment from God. *What--,* you want to interfere with what God is doing or what God is teaching that person?

When this is perverted, some actively look for others who are less fortunate than themselves so they can feel good about themselves. Of course, if this type of person doesn't feel good about him or herself already, then they are not BLESSED in the first place. They are lacking a certain peace. If they are worried, self-conscious, feel the world is up against them, looking at them, they don't have that peace of God, they are not blessed.

This person who is looking for someone to be better than is not of God, they are from the kingdom of darkness. Their soul needs some healing, deliverance, restoration. No one who felt superior to anyone came to that altar and gave of their substance; they were all moved with compassion from the heart of God.

People who are not moved by the Spirit of God have hardened hearts. Those people walk around with their nose in the air, and they don't give. Those who want to lord their wealth, property or status over others are not behaving in a Godly way. This is a perversion of what God intended, and it is not of God.

If we seek out or happen to discover the conditions of others and find them needy or lacking, then we give as the Word says. We do something about it as the Word says. We help them, as instructed by the Lord. I saw nowhere in the Bible where anyone asked Jesus for anything and if given an instruction and they followed it, that Jesus didn't bless them, or give them what they asked for.

Anyone asking for bread should not receive a stone.

As God has blessed us, as God has multiplied us, then we may share with others as the Spirit leads. This is another reason why you need YOUR OWN relationship with GOD and know how to pray and also hear God. What? Are you going to call your intercessor when it's offering time and you're at church? No, you need to hear God for yourself.

Are you going to text your prayer buddy and ask if you should give, and how much? Of course not. Ask God yourself and hear God, do what God says.

You need to HEAR GOD for yourself and use Wisdom.

Life

Job was a very successful man who gave props to God for his success. (Job 1:10). Job said that because he was blessed of God, he had all that he had, and he had a lot. Among the things Job had were 10 children. Right there we see that Job was doing the things this book is about, being fruitful and multiplying.

- He was married.
- He was being fruitful within the marriage.
- And Job was multiplying.

Job wasn't just having kids, even though ten is a lot, Job was multiplying;

he had cattle and sheep and goats and oxen and donkeys. Everything about Job was prospering.

Take note, Job wasn't just doing that on his own, he was doing it in conjunction, in relationship with God. When you see a church where there are no new members, or members keep leaving, the *spirit of death* is over that place. Job was prospering in his cattle and new life was coming forth. There was no death over Job's ranch, before the devil came and smote it. Instead, the light of God was shining on Job and oil was pouring forth like a river and his steps were covered with butter. Everything was smooth.

I was in a church that for years no one was pregnant, and no one had a baby… there was no life in that church; it was dead. I was sent there for a season. There was a day, however, when I advised everyone that I was praying for multiplication and if they were doing something that they didn't want to multiply to stop it! And then I prayed. One couple got pregnant right away.

Multiplying means LIFE. GOD IS LIFE. Jesus said I am the WAY, the TRUTH and the LIFE. Reproduction and *multiplication* **prove** LIFE.

Job was priesting for his children by giving sacrifices to God after his children's regular *feast days*. Please note that these were his children's feast days, the Bible doesn't indicate that they were the feast days of the Lord, but only peculiar to Job's children.

Job was maintaining the altar with regular sacrifices. That is how you stay connected spiritually to God. In this way, it is more blessed to give, to put a bullock or two on the altar, to sacrifice. It is more blessed for you or for me to be connected spiritually to God than not. It is more blessed for us to be and stay connected to God. We do this by regular sacrifice.

A dead church has a dead or ungodly altar. Because Job was married, and had found favor in the eyes of God, and had 10 children, and was in multiplication--, even his cattle were multiplying, GOD had to fulfill His end of that verse and also multiply Job all the more. There is another promise for our children when these conditions are met--, possessing the gates of enemies.

More Blessed

We become *more* blessed because we are ratifying covenant with God, or restoring covenant, or reconfirming covenant with GOD. We are blessed even more for giving to God because the lesser is made better by the stronger. God is the greatest power; He will never be defeated. We are lesser and we NEED GOD, we need HIM every day all day. So, we are *more blessed* when we give to establish or re-establish covenant with God.

We are *more blessed* when we receive deliverance from our offerings in any number of ways ---, one sure way is that we affirm that JESUS IS LORD, of our life and also of our MONEY. By putting money on the altar, it brings Jesus to the Throne of our hearts.

When we receive, we receive in this world and from this world. We are supposed to be **in** this world but not *of* it. Therefore, when we give--, especially at a Godly Altar, we sanctify all of our increase, we bless God because He can say, ***That's my Son. That's my child— look at that one.*** Amen

We bless the work of the Lord because now there is meat in the storehouse. God can show us favor now. He can rebuke the devourer(s) and make us more blessed because we did the better thing and that was to sanctify that Earth money and increase.

We did the better thing, because look how much our little bit can bless when added to others from the House of God. Whatever souls are won, whatever crowns are attained, whatever poor are fed, whatever sick are being prayed for and healed, if we helped to sponsor or promote it, we share in those crowns. That makes us *MORE blessed*.

Not only that, but we also knocked Mammon off the throne of our hearts and enthroned the Lord God, which we need to do daily, often, not just once when we get saved at age 13 or 15, or whenever.

He Went *Through*

Yeah, Job went through it--, chapters and chapters of *through*, but God made him **more blessed** in the end. Saints of God, sometimes we might need to go through, but know that our latter end will be greater than the former, if we stay in the LORD and stay connected to the Godly Altar that we are submitted to or have been assigned to.

So the Lord blessed the latter end of Job more than his beginning: for he had fourteen thousand sheep, and six thousand camels, and a thousand yoke of oxen, and a thousand she asses.
(Job 42:12)

Also, in the end, after Job had sent up offerings and prayed for his friends, a banquet was held where relatives and friends that had stood afar off from Job came to feast with him. The Word says they each bought him a piece of silver or gold; God did a Go Fund Me for Job, which I like to call a God Fund Me.

Saints, notice that those people had silver and gold that they could give Job **while** Job was going through, but in their Wisdom and possibly instruction from God, they did not give to a man who was under judgment from God, or *looked* like he was under judgment from God.

- Does that answer for you why you can't find your friends when you're down and out?

- Does that answer for you why you can't get a bank loan when you need a bank loan?

- Does it answer why you are only offered loans when you don't need them?

It's spiritual – when you're going *through*, you may have reproach on you; you are not blessed and no one wants to be around you, really. No one wants to help you. if you look like you're not blessed, no one wants to be around you. if you look like, act like, or sound like you are not blessed, no one wants to be around you. Sorry.

People naturally want to be around folks who are blessed. This doesn't make it right; I'm just talking about human nature. In Christ, we are supposed to be better than that; we are to do what Jesus would do. Just as He would run to the weary, the sick and the weak--, the blind and the halt, that is ministry, folks. That's what we are supposed to do, unless God says don't. **To know if a person is under judgment, check with God.**

When you're going *through,* you may be distraught. You may look distraught. You may want to talk about it, vent – friends will be hard to find --- you'd better trust me on this… your fair-weather friends will be hard to find. Maybe they don't have a heart for it, they don't know what to say, they have no counseling spirit or no compassion. Many times, their excuse is, *I don't know what to say*, so they disappear.

But go ahead and get blessed. Get a raise at work. Throw a party or treat everyone for brunch – you will have friends popping out of the woodwork. Your worldly, carnal, fake, fair-weather friends will find you when you are doing well. When you are feeling good, settled, and peaceful, people will find you.

Peace is a blessing. It's part of the blessing where God makes you rich and He adds no sorrow with it. When God restores the Peace in your life, especially after a financial or other storm, it is peace indeed, peace like a river, peace in every area of a man's life; peace that surpasses understanding. Now, that is a blessing. That's built into being blessed.

Not only that, **PEACE** draws wealth. Wealth shouldn't be drawing the peace, else you are serving Mammon.

WAR and irritation and anger and antagonism repel WEALTH, they repel blessings.

It was when that diabolical, devil-induced storm was over that money and wealth were released to Job again.

Peace is part and parcel of the blessing.

Job is very rich, a man of honor, himself and you bring a worthy gift to a man of honor, so the friends and family came with the God Fund Me silver and gold.

The Multiplication

In the Bible, God didn't promise any unmarried man that He would **multiply** him. This could be why our parents and elders keep asking us when we are of age, when are we going to get married. We think it's because they want us to settle down and get off the streets. We may think it is because they want grandchildren, and they may think it is because they want grandchildren. But there are things of God, things in this life that just *are*, the way they are. Those things are understood, especially by parents and grandparents.

So, somewhere on the screensaver of a wise person's mind, especially a wise parent, that mental screensaver says my child needs to get married and have a family. They may think it is because they don't want their child to be alone, live alone, grow old alone, or die alone. Perhaps it is all that. But God knows the deeper reason for any and all of what any wise person, any person imbued with Wisdom and knowledge may think, act on, or speak.

In marriage is the blessing. In marriage is the favor. He who finds a wife finds a good thing and obtains *favor* from God.

In marriage is <u>multiplication</u>. God said, the Word said: ***In multiplying, I will multiply you.*** **That multiplication is not just for marriage, it is for your entire life.**

And it is echoed in Hebrews:

...saying, "I WILL SURELY BLESS YOU AND I WILL SURELY

MULTIPLY YOU."
(Hebrews 6:14 AMP)

In order to multiply or prepare for such, a husband and wife have to assemble themselves together. Ideally, as they are together, God speaks. God speaks when they are praying. God speaks when they are working. God speaks when they are taking a meal or relaxing together, or handling *kingdom business*. When God speaks, things are set in order, things also assemble themselves properly. When God speaks things improve and settle and have Peace. When God speaks, things multiply and they multiply properly. When God speaks the right things multiply, and then God multiplies **you**. The right things multiply, including finances.

Why aren't you multiplying financially? Because you aren't multiplying in the natural. No, I'm not saying that God will pay you to have children, I'm saying there is reward in obedience to the Word of God.

Some males think that women want to marry them for their money. What they don't realize is that they will have so much more when they obey God and get married (to the right person) because the Word says so. *In multiplying, I will multiply you.*

As long as *be fruitful and mul*tiply is working in the Earth, and it still is--, it can be captured and appropriated even by the dark side. It is why one odd spot or cell on someone's skin can replicate itself and become something that a doctor should remove and probably biopsy. It is why one ant in your kitchen needs to be gone immediately, if not there may be an entire colony marching in as if they pay the mortgage or the rent at your house.

Even the dark side knows that things can multiply, but we are going to stay upright in our walk before the Lord and we are going to give sacrifices on Godly altars so we can get the blessing and the multiplication.

That ye might walk worthy of the Lord unto all pleasing, being fruitful in every good work, and increasing in the knowledge of God; (Colossians1:10)

There is an order to this. Let all things be done decently and in order. Abraham and Sarah multiplied their own way at first and created the flesh child, Ishmael. We have to do it God's way, in God's order. That put at risk the child of Promise, Isaac, and delayed Isaac's arrival on Earth. It was 25 years from the time God told Abraham that he would have a child of Promise to actually having Isaac. Abraham and Sarah kept doing things counter to the Promise, but God blessed them anyway, and still kept covenant and kept the faith with them. Thank You, Jesus.

Seedtime & Harvest

Abraham sowed a seed. Sarah received it. Isaac finally got here.

As long as the Earth remains there will be seedtime and harvest. Seed is one, it is planted, grows and reaches maturity. Harvest happens when *multiplication has happened after it has reached maturity.* One seed can produce manifold of itself, so much after its own kind.

The first mystery that must be solved is seed **time**. Man can have a problem with Time, or he can figure out how to make time work for him. When is seedtime? When is it time to plant? At church sometimes, it is when the pastor says so. As we believe the pastor is hearing from God, seed time is actually when God says so. It is also when God says, *Sow*. All things decently and in order.

God has established so many ways for man to know time, times, and seasons that he needs to pay attention, so he doesn't as Jesus said in the Gospels miss his time of visitation. He that observes the wind will never sow. We have to be diligent and obedient and be listening for the Word of God to hear what thus saith the Lord. If you plan to multiply or have multiplication, you will have to sow. And, you have to know when to sow, where to sow, and how to sow.

Farmer Brown planted a seed, and it grew a thousand-fold, or a million-fold of itself and now it is time to harvest. The Lord of the Harvest reaps in multiplication. Not only does He help you reap, but He is there to sanctify your harvest, to bless what you have harvested so that your increase will be holy.

If He doesn't--, if you don't allow Him to bless your increase then your increase is not blessed and therefore you aren't either. If it is not blessed, then it is not a blessing of the Lord, it is NOT a blessing of the LORD of the Harvest. The blessings of the Lord maketh rich and He adds no sorrow with it.

He says, *In blessing I will bless you and in multiplying I will multiply you.*

Saints of God, if God is not blessing your increase, then you cannot put the label of **Blessing of the Lord** on your increases or harvests.

The blessings of the Lord are the only ones that maketh rich AND add no sorrow.

So, a person could work and work, even their fingers to the bone, and not be made rich. Or, a person could see increase in their bank accounts, but if God didn't **bless** what you got, then there will be sorrow. Sorrow may come upon that wealth and the life of the person who is trying, without God, to hold onto that wealth. Without God a person could be well off, but miserable in any number of ways.

Still, to keep one's wealth, we need God because the enemies of God are also your enemies, and they are coming for that wealth.

Jesus had Judas hold the bag for His ministry, that was by divine construct; and that was by divine plan, but unless you let Jesus hold the bag for your harvests, your gains, your increase and your money, then it is not blessed and you haven't multiplied, or you won't keep what you harvested by your own hand, if you are leaving God out of it.

The wealth of the wicked is laid up for the just.

In that harvest and in that transaction of letting God **bless you and letting God bless** what you have just received, YOU multiply. And, in **your** multiplying, GOD says He will *multiply* you.

One seed, much harvest. **Multiplication**.

Sure, He will come for one, but God expects multiplication.

In soul winning, God expects many – many sons, many daughters, many converts.

In planting, sowing and restoration by multiplication we expect the replenishing of good things, things that are lovely and have purpose and good report. God said, *Be fruitful and multiply and replenish the Earth.*

If God gives you a seed, then as Lord of the Harvest, He comes for the harvest, He comes at harvest time. One of the ways that God teaches us time and the timing of things, is by the celestial bodies, by the seasons and one of those seasons is the harvest. Who doesn't know when it's harvest time?

But it's one of the ways that God knows when to expect your tithe—at harvest time. This is why Cain couldn't trick God. Cain brought his offering, but I don't think he brought it on time. (My opinion.)

At harvest time, God is not coming back for the original seed --- *Lord, I knew you are a hard man, so I hid the one talent you gave me when you left. I didn't want to lose it, so here it is.*

Jesus rebuked the wicked servant, saying something like, *Get away from me you wicked servant* (Matthew 25:14-30). That unproductive man did not *multiply* what had been given to him.

Speaking of converts, as soon as you win a soul to Christ, what do you do? You pray and you ask God's blessing, and for God's hand to be over that person's life, and you hand that person over to the Lord. You give that soul to the Lord, to follow **Christ** and become His disciple, not your own *follower*.

That's what you do with all increase--, the increase of souls, increase of revenue, increase of money---, increase of everything. Hand what you're supposed to hand over to God so He can bless it.

In blessing, God says, **I will bless you, and in multiplying**, **I will multiply you.**

We need God in the process of planting, growing, watering and harvesting both souls and also our metaphorical gardens that we tend as we work our 9 to 5's.

Why?

- Because the wild birds come for the seeds before they can even germinate.
- Because there are many types of soil, and the seed will respond in various ways depending on the soil.

- Because while men sleep the enemy sows weeds into a garden or a field.
- And because when it is time to harvest here come the enemies of God. Every year the Midianites tore up the crops of the Israelites, so they had no harvest. That's what the enemy does.

The sower sows the seed, the Word is the seed, and the expectation is to reap souls for the Kingdom of Heaven. The sower is blessed, he is already blessed by God, who has spoken over him, saying it is good. NOW, sow your seed, whatever kind of seed it is, and for whatever you are sowing for.

The sower that sows the seed in the natural, whether it is with his spouse, or in a garden outside, or wherever he works his 9 to 5. That sower is blessed, to even have a seed. He is already been blessed by God who is saying over him, BE

FRUITFUL and multiply. God is not going to tell some halfway something, or *sort-of* thing to multiply. God has determined that a thing is good and He blessed it, **before** it is time to multiply that thing.

Now is the time to sow, this is where you sow. He has spoken over him, saying you are blessed, it is good, that is, you are blessed. If you are blessed person who is sowing, then you should expect a good harvest. If you are cursed person who is sowing, expect to receive nothing or curses or a harvest of shame.

God didn't say to any unmarried man that he would multiply him. God doesn't create rich playboys – the devil does.

Be blessed by finding favor in God by marrying whom God tells you to marry. The blessing is in the marriage. **The favor from God is because you found your wife**. Bless the LORD. Bless your spouse. Honor God, be fruitful and multiply.

- Then AS YOU multiply, and because you multiply, GOD will also *multiply you.*
- Expect **multiplication** because God said so.
- Have faith for **multiplication** because the Word said so.
- Look for **multiplication** because we are blessed, you are in covenant with God and in blessing He will bless you and in Multiplying, He will multiply you.
- Look for **multiplication**, be *multiplied* and then the Lord will add to that and also Multiply you, His way, in the Name of Jesus.

Jesus was the firstborn of many brethren and there is no record of Him getting married and multiplying. Jesus was all man and all God, so He had other ways of multiplying, as does God.

Provision

Thy wife shall be as a fruitful vine by the sides of thine house: thy children like olive plants round about thy table.
(Psalm 128:3)

God is not the type to give you lots of children with no way to take care of them. He is a God of provision. God would not send a child on a journey with no means to be sustained; He's not cruel.

I don't believe God would give a person even one child with no way to take care of that child. In the Bible, I saw no examples of such unless there was judgment on the person or the people, and there was, for example, famine in the land. God gave so much advance notice when a famine would come, and He always gave the people a way out of judgment by repentance and turning back to Him so the curse would not come upon the land. Many times, God gave people **years** to repent before He struck them down, or struck the Earth with a curse, pestilence, or famine.

Note here that God says, *I* **will surely bless you and I will surely multiply you.** That certainly means you have to do things God's way. God did not say go out and find baby mama after baby mama and roll your stones all over everywhere to make yourself a "papa." God did not say multiply yourself by finding baby daddy after baby daddy. God said HE would multiply you. And where God makes a plan, He gives a vision. Where there is a Godly vision, there is provision.

Sexual sin leads to instability in all aspects of life. If you want a miserable life and a poor or impoverished child, get that child through sexual sin. Not only will your life be or become unstable, the child and up to your 4th generation will suffer because of that.

When you go ahead of God and get a thousand kids, not acknowledging the Lord, the children become a curse to you rather than a blessing.

And as for Ishmael, I have heard thee: Behold, I have blessed him, and will make him fruitful, and will multiply him exceedingly; twelve princes shall he beget, and I will make him a great nation.
(Genesis 17:20)

The above verse proves that you can take multiplication into your own hands and make a mess of things as Sarah and Abrahm did with Hagar.

On the other hand, if you do it God's way you will get the results that God says you will get and there will be no sorrow added. Please don't fall under condemnation if you did it some other way than God's way. Turn to Him and He can forgive, cleanse, restore and lift you up out of any situation or circumstance.

Multiplying

And God blessed them,
saying, Be fruitful, and multiply, and fill
the waters in the seas, and let fowl
multiply in the earth. (Genesis 1:22)

And God blessed them, and God said
unto them, Be fruitful, and multiply, and
replenish the earth, and subdue it: and
have dominion over the fish of the sea,
and over the fowl of the air, and over
every living thing that moveth upon the
earth. (Genesis 1:28)

Bring forth with thee every living thing
that is with thee, of all flesh, both of
fowl, and of cattle, and of every
creeping thing that creepeth upon the
earth; that they may breed abundantly
in the earth, and be fruitful, and
multiply upon the earth. (Genesis 8:17)

As said, God can turn off Multiplication and He did when there was the Flood. Not only was Multiplication turned off, but it was also undone. People were lost, lands, crops, everything. Scholars said that the Flood and the waters lasted about a year. That should get everything good and drowned that God wanted drowned. So, Noah and his family and all the animals that he took upon the Ark landed and disembarked, and God gave them instructions:

And God blessed Noah and his sons, and said unto them, Be fruitful, and multiply, and replenish the earth. (Genesis 9:1)

And you, be ye fruitful, and multiply; bring forth abundantly in the earth, and multiply therein. (Genesis 9:7)

Divine Exception

We must do our part to receive multiplication; there are requirements to the covenant that we are under. We should walk upright and obey the statutes and laws of the Lord. Else, we may find ourselves under judgment, and we don't ever want to be there. We do as we should, but if we are under a bondage such as collective captivity of our family, neighborhood, city, state, or country for example, we will have to pray for exception.

God has answered prayers of exception many times. God sustained the prophet by a dirty bird in the times of famine; that was an exception. God allowed the Tribes of Israel to sojourn into

Egypt more than once to get provision for the famine back in Israel.

Spies came through the land and afterward the land was desolated, but Rahab stayed alive. Exception. Pray to God for it. Divine Exception.

When God has declared judgment, such as we see images in Isaiah; we must ask for Divine Exception.

And shall consume the glory of his forest, and of his fruitful field, both soul and body: and they shall be as when a standard-bearer fainteth. (Isaiah 10:18)

Until the spirit be poured upon us from on high, and the wilderness be a fruitful field, and the fruitful field be counted for a forest. (Isaiah 32:15)

And in Jeremiah:

And I will gather the remnant of my flock out of all countries whither I have driven them, and will bring them again to their folds; and they

shall be fruitful and increase.
(Jeremiah 23:3)

And also, in Hosea.

Though he **be fruitful** among his
brethren, an east wind shall come, the
wind of the LORD shall come up from the
wilderness, and his spring shall **be**come
dry, and his fountain shall **be** dried up:
he shall spoil the treasure of all pleasant
vessels.(Hosea 13:15)

Repent to get out of the judgment.
Repent and do warfare to get out of a curse
that was not sent by God because of your
disobedience.

And there shall cleave nought of the
cursed thing to thine hand: that
the LORD may turn from the fierceness
of his anger, and shew thee mercy, and
have compassion upon thee,
and multiply thee, as he hath sworn
unto thy fathers; (Deuteronomy 13:17)

And it shall come to pass, that as
the LORD rejoiced over you to do you
good, and to **multiply** you; so
the LORD will rejoice over you to destroy

you, and to bring you to nought; and ye
shall be plucked from off the land
whither thou goest to possess it.
(Deuteronomy 28:63)

Not Multiplying

Folks, this is why barrenness is about much more than whether or not you have children, but when you willfully do not have children, you are disobeying what was spoken to _**all**_ the people, and also to Creation in the first chapter of Genesis.

If you are not multiplying, then the promise of God multiplying you is not yours. Have you noticed that those who don't have children chase business and finances to the max? Have you noticed that those who chase finances sometimes miss the window to having children? Either is a sign of barrenness; either affects the other.

Having finances, and finances only still speaks of barrenness. Having children and being broke is still a form of barrenness. Barrenness applies to the productivity and fruitfulness of **all** aspects of a man's life.

Not only that, being married and drinking waters out of your own cistern--, being faithful to the spouse of your youth will protect you from so much captivity, especially captivity that spawns from sexual sins and illicit relations.

It is better to marry than to burn.

Multiply the Person

When multiplication is working, what you touch multiplies. What you speak to multiplies. It is as though a *spirit of multiplication* has been gifted to you. That's a real thing because you've met people who everything they touch seems to prosper. And you've met others who tear of everything they put their hands to.

When a guy breaks every electronic device that he touches: he has cursed hands.

The person who betters and increases everything he touches has blessed hands.

If God has blessed you and also made you a blessing what you touch becomes blessed. What you bless multiplies. Jesus prayed and fishes and loaves multiplied and fed the multitude. The prayers of prophets in the Old Testament multiplied corn and meal and jars of oil. When <u>you</u> pray, what multiplies?

And the angel of the LORD said unto her, I will **multiply** thy seed exceedingly, that it shall not be numbered for multitude. (Genesis 16:10)

And I will make my covenant between me and thee, and will **multiply** thee exceedingly. (Genesis 17:2)

When God is multiplying something, He expects it to be something good. Something established. Something that He is in covenant with. And God said, over and again, "**It is good, it is good, it is good.**" *Now multiply that.*

When you are out in these streets doing whatever and becoming whatever, you cannot just proclaim yourself as good, although many of us do and then decide it is time to duplicate or replicate yourself. Unless God said so, it may not be good and what you will create, even though it's cute and innocent and smells good most of the time, will be like you. We all reproduce after our kind.

When God says, *It is time*, it is time. Are you staying prayerful or are you just letting nature take its course? Nature's course is default to this Earth and the devil is running that.

Remember Abraham, Isaac, and Israel, thy servants, to whom thou swarest by thine own self, and saidst unto them, I will **multiply** your seed as the stars of heaven, and all this land that I have spoken of will I give unto your seed, and they shall inherit it for ever.
(Exodus 32:13)

If God is multiplying the thing then you are in the perfect position. Have you been blessing God? That is maintaining your relationship with Him?

Then He will bless you and in blessing, He also declares the season of your multiplication your readiness, your soul prosperity, according to the time of life, and He will multiply you.

Pray to the Lord for the multiplication anointing. That will come after God has formed you, breathed into you, made you a living soul, declared that you are good, blessed you and has seen that you are obedient to be fruitful and multiply. Then God multiplies you. Once God knows He can trust you, you receive the anointing to bless others. You receive the anointing to multiply. You receive an anointing to be a multiplier and continuously be multiplied in everything you are involved in; in everything you touch.

Folks, this is the pattern if you are looking to bring righteous seed to the Earth.

Blessed to Be A Blessing

For I will have respect unto you, and
make you fruitful, and **multiply** you,
and establish my covenant with you.
(Leviticus 26:9)

And he will love thee, and bless thee,
and multiply thee: he will also bless the
fruit of thy womb, and the fruit of thy
land, thy corn, and thy wine, and thine
oil, the increase of thy kine, and the
flocks of thy sheep, in the land which he
sware unto thy fathers to give thee.
(Deuteronomy 7:13)

All the commandments which I
command thee this day shall ye observe
to do, that ye may live, and multiply,
and go in and possess the land which
the LORD sware unto your fathers.
(Deuteronomy 8:1)

And when thy herds and thy
flocks multiply, and thy silver and thy
gold is multiplied, and all that thou hast
is multiplied; (Deuteronomy 8:13)

And the LORD thy God will bring thee
into the land which thy fathers
possessed, and thou shalt possess it; and
he will do thee good, and multiply thee
above thy fathers. (Deuteronomy 30:5)

In that I command thee this day to love
the LORD thy God, to walk in his ways,
and to keep his commandments and his
statutes and his judgments, that thou
mayest live and **multiply**: and
the LORD thy God shall bless thee in the
land whither thou goest to possess it.
(Deuteronomy 30:16)

And out of them shall proceed
thanksgiving and the voice of them that
make merry: and I will **multiply** them,
and they shall not be few; I will also
glorify them, and they shall not be small.
(Jeremiah 30:19)

As the host of heaven cannot be
numbered, neither the sand of the sea
measured: so will I **multiply** the seed of

David my servant, and the Levites that minister unto me. (Jeremiah 33:22)

Lord Restore

And I will multiply upon you man and beast; and they shall increase and bring fruit: and I will settle you after your old estates, and will do better unto you than at your beginnings: and ye shall know that I am the LORD. (Ezekiel 36:11)

And I will multiply the fruit of the tree, and the increase of the field, that ye shall receive no more reproach of famine among the heathen.
(Ezekiel 36:30)

Moreover I will make a covenant of peace with them; it shall be an everlasting covenant with them: and I will place them, and **multiply** them, and will set my sanctuary in the midst of them for evermore. (Ezekiel 37:26)

Sometimes in our ignorance, disobedience, and rebellion, we've done it all wrong. Sometimes we've been led astray. Sometimes we wandered off on our own. We must, now that we know better, ask the Lord to help us get right before Him again.

- Lord, restore the years, redeem the Time, in the Name of Jesus.
- Lord, because of my own sins or shortcomings, do not let anyone who is supposed to bless me or be a blessing to me give what is mine to the cruel, in the Name of Jesus.

In Multiplying

Saying, Surely blessing I will bless thee,
and multiplying I will multiply thee.
(Hebrews 6:4)

First there is addition--, one plus one--, man plus woman. After addition, then comes the multiplication. When there is one, that is only ½ a replacement. When there is 2 that is replacement. Multiplication doesn't happen until there is at least another one. At least. I'm not saying those who don't have at least three children are disobedient to God because in the creation of one, many are multiplied, such as cells, atoms, and molecules, on the micro level. Without multiplication and replication a new human could not be formed.

> Now he that ministereth seed to the sower both minister bread for your food, and **multiply** your seed sown, and increase the fruits of your righteousness;) (2 Corinthians 9:10)

Divorce

Divorce is *un*Multiplication. It could be one of the reasons why God hates divorce. It is broken covenant, and God hates broken Godly covenant. Broken covenant is also in direct opposition to *Be Fruitful and Multiply* because multiplication in humans does not happen alone; it takes two--, not three, not three or more, it takes two.

God takes pleasure in anyone who breaks evil covenants and will come to your cause when you pray and ask Him to help you break evil covenants made in error, those made in rebellion, and evil soul ties.

In marriage, however, what God has joined together no man can tear apart, or *put asunder* as the Word says. I believe that if God put a marriage together that couple can't get divorced, and they won't.

That marriages seem to break up so easily says to me that God wasn't in it, or it wasn't a Godly covenant. In some cases, there is no covenant at all—when only one person is in the marriage and the other person is only loosely associated with the other person for whatever selfish reasons, there is no agreement, there is no covenant. It takes two.

Sometimes God is not in what some folks believe is a covenant--, anywhere. Sometimes God **was** in it, but one or both parties turned their backs on God. Outside assaults may come, strange women, strange men are sent to marriages and the egotistical think they are *pulling* while the wise stand up and pray for their mate and their marriage.

Where is your mind? Is it on marriage and staying married, being a blessing to your spouse and family? Is it on being fruitful and multiplying? Meditate on the foundational Scripture of this book that in *multiplying*, **God will *multiply* you**. If that doesn't make you want to obey God and walk in His blessings, then you most likely need deliverance for your flesh, because flesh and the pleasures of it are most often what pulls a person from their marriage.

Don't be the devil's victim. Do you realize by divorcing how much *multiplication* you will lose out on? That's not the whole reason to stay married, because you also can't fake a marriage. God is not mocked. Be married and stay married because God said so; be obedient. In that obedience there are great rewards. Outside of obedience, there is great loss.

Who is to say if you will ever recover from that loss? Like, *ever*?

Murder

Divorce is hard; divorce is foul, but the ultimate in non-proliferation is doing what Cain did, murder.

I mention this because God finally allowed Old Testament divorce because the men were killing their wives so they could get new ones. Folks, the Bible is true and some of its recounts are ruthless.

Even natural man has laws that prohibit a person from prospering from his crimes. Don't be complicit in the murder of your own prosperity and your own destiny.

Have you ever noticed that married, stable people live longer, usually? Have you ever noticed that married people who have not had multiple divorces have better lives, are healthier, usually? Have you ever noticed that people who stay married and are really married and don't get divorces have golden years, better retirements that haven't been raided by lawyers and they have more money when it is all said and done to live on and to leave their children and their *children's* children. These people, who have obeyed God's laws and respected covenant have become established by God and are not unstable as those who are out in the streets in sin, especially sexual sin.

Many things can murder a marriage. That is sad too, since a dead marriage cannot multiply, and if you don't multiply within the covenant of marriage, then God won't multiply you.

Death

We talked about the dead church earlier, the one where there are no new members, there are no marriages really, and there are no babies being born of anyone in the church. That's death.

Man cannot replicate or multiply in death. People are not given to be wives or husbands in death. Angels do not replicate themselves.

This is how more demons are created. Does the devil make demons and more devils? No, he recruits evil human agents to do his bidding. Then, there are synthetics – hybrids from entanglements that should not be.

When the death of multiplication has come, or worse, when it never had a chance to start, we see that we haven't followed God's rules that all the people who say they are Christians are supposed to have heard.

When children are born out of wedlock, out of situationships, out of witchcraft and trickery, the devil is having a field day. Worse, is when a baby is born out of God's order and then you see the parent, usually a single, struggle and struggle, it is obvious that God is not multiplying them spiritually. Of course, its is because they multiplied *physically* without God or outside of God's plan and the hand of God is tied to multiply them. As discussed, when we multiply God's way, He also multiplies us, spiritually so we lack nothing and have all things pertaining to life and godliness.

Some may say you get a husband, and that husband provides for the family. Say what you will, a wife and a husband having a baby is God's order and if they do what God says, God's way as they multiply, God multiplies them. I am saying that God gives that man the ability to prosper financially if he is the breadwinner so he can take care of his family.

The single man may not have that same success. Have you noticed that companies promote married men versus single men more often? You and the company may think it is because that man is deemed more stable. Perhaps it is. The man who is single and out in the world, most often is committing sexual sins. Sexual sins make people unstable. So there is that.

Instability such as men chasing women, women chasing men. Folks running after each other, folks hiding from each other. Folks stalking each other's houses and jobs. Folks moving to get away from someone that they never should have slept with in the first place.

Folks taking others to court for child support. Custody battles – People of God, all that is instability and drama! No decent business wants to deal with that or have an employee who is constantly in disagreements or fights with exes, be they ex-spouses or ex dates.

God is not the author of this confusion, and He is neither blessing nor multiplying that. A man can be so unstable in his life that he can negatively affect the company that he begins to work for. Many of these companies are not Christian companies and they don't even want that drama, so how much do you think a Christian firm will be able to endure? How much do you think God will bless the unstable?

Yeah, you may have to go through first, hopefully not as bad as Job, but God can establish you, bless you and multiply you if you are in Him and obey His rules and laws.

But the God of all grace, who hath called us unto his eternal glory by Christ

Jesus, after that ye have suffered a while, make you perfect, stablish, strengthen, you. (1 Peter 5:10)

Prayers

1. Lord, have Mercy on me a sinner, forgive me for my sins and the sins of my parents and my ancestors, remove all iniquity from our family line, in the Name of Jesus.

2. Lord, thank You for the commandment and the authority to **Be Fruitful and Multiply**, I hear it, I hear You, Lord, I want to walk in that, in the Name of Jesus.

3. I love You, Lord, let me walk in Your ways, keep Your commandments, statutes, and judgments, that I may live, be blessed, and multiply, in the Name of Jesus.

4. LORD, bless me out of Zion, wherever I live and wherever you send me to live, in the Name of Jesus.

5. Lord, let me find favor in Your sight, in the Name of Jesus.

6. Lord, let me be blessed by You, in the Name of Jesus.

7. In blessing, Lord, bless me, bless me indeed.

8. Lord, I possess my possessions, in the Name of Jesus.

9. The blessings of the LORD maketh rich and He adds no sorrow with it, in the Name of Jesus.

10. Lord, let me legally be fruitful and multiply according to Your Word, according to Your commandment from Genesis, in the Name of Jesus.

11. In multiplying, Lord, multiply me, increase me, in the Name of Jesus.

12. Lord, keep me away from secret sins that hinder my ability to receive what You have prepared and sent me, in the Name of Jesus.
13. Lord, by Your Holy Spirit, help me to keep covenant with You, in the Name of Jesus.
14. Lord, if I am not married, send my covenant spouse today, so that I may be in line to be blessed, to find favor, to multiply and to be multiplied, in the Name of Jesus.
15. Lord, if I am married, let us keep covenant with You and with one another, and let us be fruitful and multiply or continue to do so, to the Praise of Your Glory. Amen.
16. Thank You, Lord that all things are done decently and in order, in the Name of Jesus.
17. Thank You that you are the God of more than enough; thank You,

Lord for provision to meet the
vision, for our family, in the Name
of Jesus.

18. In blessing, Lord, bless me, in the
Name of Jesus.

19. In blessing, Lord, bless me, in the
Name of Jesus.

20. In blessing, Lord, bless me, in the
Name of Jesus.

21. In multiplying, Lord, multiply me,
in the Name of Jesus.

22. In multiplying, Lord, multiply me,
in the Name of Jesus.

23. In multiplying, Lord, multiply me,
in the Name of Jesus.

24. I seal these declarations across
every realm, dimension, era and
timeline, past present and future,
to infinity. I seal them with the
Holy Spirit of Promise and the
Blood of Jesus.

25. All retaliation intended or
attempted against these prayers

fail and backfire to infinity, in the Name of Jesus.

AMEN.

Dear Reader

Thank you for acquiring, reading, and sharing this book. I pray the Lord will bless you and keep you. I pray the Favor of the Lord will find you. I pray that you walk uprightly before the Lord and obey Him. I pray that as you multiply the Lord will multiply you.

In the Name of Jesus,

Amen.

Dr. Marlene Miles

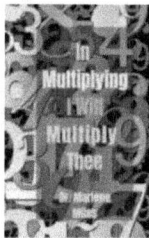

Other books by this author

AK: *The Adventures of the Agape Kid*

AMONG SOME THIEVES

Ancestral Powers https://a.co/d/9prTyFf

Backstabbers https://a.co/d/gi8iBxf

Barrenness, *Prayers Against*
https://a.co/d/feUltIs

Battlefield of Marriage, *The*

Blindsided: *Has the Old Man
Bewitched You?* https://a.co/d/5O2fLLR

Break Free from Collective Captivity

Caged Life https://a.co/d/0eKxbU9H

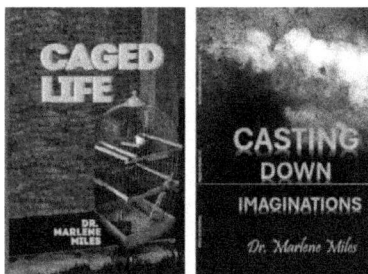

Casting Down Imaginations
https://a.co/d/1UxlLqa

Church Craft: Witchcraft In the
Church

Churchzilla, The Wanna-Be, Supposed-to-be Bride of Christ

Curses of Blind Men

Demonic Cobwebs (prayerbook)

Demonic Time Bombs

Demons Hate Questions

Devil Loves Trauma, *The*

Devil Weapons: Unforgiveness, Bitterness,...

The Devourers: *Thieves of Darkness 2*

Do Not Swear by the Moon

Don't Refuse Me, Lord (4 book series)
https://a.co/d/idP34LG

Dream Defilement

The Emptiers: *Thieves of Darkness, 1*
https://a.co/d/5I4n5mc

Every Evil Arrow
https://a.co/d/afgRkiA

Evil Touch https://a.co/d/gSGGpS1

Failed Assignment
https://a.co/d/3CXtjZY

Fantasy Spirit Spouse
https://a.co/d/hW7oYbX

FAT Demons (The): *Breaking Demonic Curses*

The Fold (5-book series)

- The Fold (Book 1)
- Name Your Seed (Book 2)
- The Poor Attitudes of Money (3)
- Do Not Orphan Your Seed (4)
- For the Sake of the Gospel (5)
- My Sowing Journal

Gang Ups: *Touch Not God's Anointed*

got HEALING? Verses for Life

got LOVE? Verses for Life

got HOPE? Verses for Life

got money? https://a.co/d/g2av41N

How to Dental Assist

How to Dental Assist2: Be Productive, Not Wasteful

I Take It Back

In Multiplying, I Will Multiply Thee

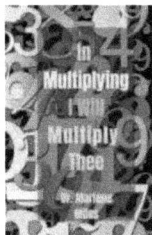

Legacy (book 3 of the Upgrade Series)

Let Me Have A Dollar's Worth
https://a.co/d/h8F8XgE

Level the Playing Field
https://www.youtube.com/watch?v=BfF-TX1EWNQ

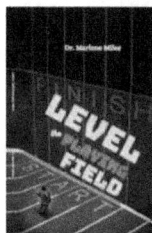

Living for the NOW of God

Lose My Location
https://a.co/d/crD6mV9

Man Safari, *The*

Marriage Ed. Rules of Engagement & Marriage

Made Perfect in Love

Money Hunters: Beware of Those

Money on the Altar https://a.co/d/4EqJ2Nr

Mulberry Tree https://a.co/d/9nR9rRb

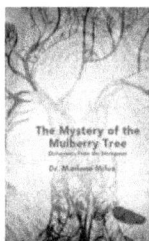

Motherboard (The)~ *Soul Prosperity Series*

Name Your Seed

Occupy: *Until I Return*

Plantation Souls

Players Gonna Play

Power Money: Nine Times the Tithe
https://a.co/d/gRt41gy

The Power of Wealth *(forthcoming)*

Powers Above

Repent of Visiting Evil Altars
https://a.co/d/3n3Zjwx

The Robe, *Part 1, The Lessons of Joseph*

The Robe, *The Lessons of Joseph* Part II,

Seasons of Grief

Seasons of Waiting

Seasons of War

Second Marriage, Third--, *Any Marriage*

https://a.co/d/6m6GN4N

Sift You Like Wheat

Six Men Short: What Has Happened to all the Men?

Son https://a.co/d/03NdPT2S

Soul Prosperity, Soul Prosperity Series Bk 3
https://a.co/d/5p8YvCN

Souls Captivity, Soul Prosperity Series Book 2

The Spirit of Poverty

StarStruck

SUNBLOCK

The Swallowers: *Thieves of Darkness*, Book 3

Take It Back

This Is NOT That: How to Keep Demons from Coming at You

Time Is of the Essence

Too Many Wives: *Why You Have Lady Problems*

Tormenting Spirits   https://a.co/d/dAogEJf

Toxic Souls

Triangular Power *(series)*

- Powers Above
- SUNBLOCK
- Do Not Swear by the Moon
- STARSTRUCK

Uncontested Doom

Unguarded Hours, *The*

Unseen Life, *The* https://a.co/d/0drZ5Ll

The Unseen Life
Dr. Matthew Stevenson

Upgrade: How to Get Out of Survival Mode

- Toxic Souls (Book 2 of series)
- Legacy (Book 3 of series)

The Wasters: *Thieves of Darkness*, Bk 2

https://a.co/d/bUvI9Jo

What Have You to Declare? What Do You Have With You from Where You've Been?

When I Was A Child, *I Prayed As a Child*

When the Devourer is Rebuked

https://a.co/d/1HVv8oq

The Wilderness Romance *(series)* This

series is about conducting a Godly relationship and marriage with someone who is a Wilderness person. It is about how to recognize it and navigate through it. These books are about how not to get caught up in such.

- *The Social Wilderness*
- *The Sexual Wilderness*
- *The Spiritual Wilderness*

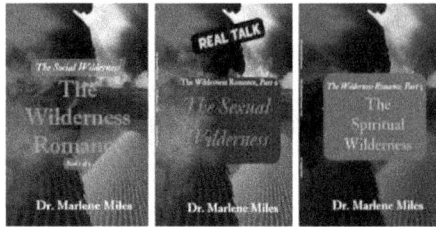

Other Series

The Fold (a series on Godly finances)
https://a.co/d/4hz3unj

Soul Prosperity Series https://a.co/d/bz2M42q

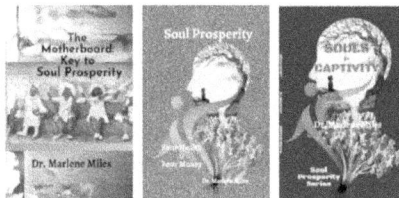

Spirit Spouse books

https://a.co/d/9VehDSo

https://a.co/d/97sKOwm

Thieves of Darkness series

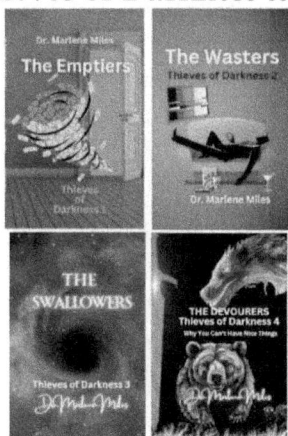

Triangular Powers https://a.co/d/aUCjAWC

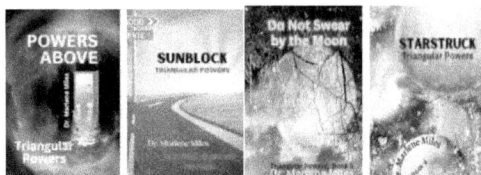

Upgrade (series) *How to Get Out of Survival Mode* https://a.co/d/aTERhXO

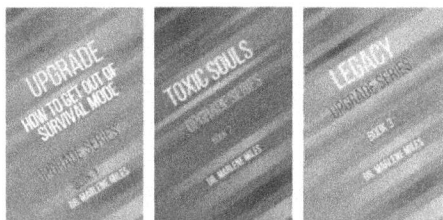

Prayer books by this author

While most books by this author have prayer points either throughout the book or at the end, there are some books that are **only** prayers. You just open up the book and pray. They are listed below:

Prayers Against Barrenness: *For Success in Business and Life*

Fruit of the Womb: *Prayers Against Barrenness*

Beauty Curses, *Warfare Prayers Against*
https://a.co/d/5Xlc20M

**Courts of Marriage: Prayers for
Marriage in the Courts of Heaven**
(prayerbook) https://a.co/d/cNAdgAq

Courtroom Warfare @ Midnight
(prayerbook) https://a.co/d/5fc7Qdp

Demonic Cobwebs *(prayerbook)*
https://a.co/d/fp9Oa2H

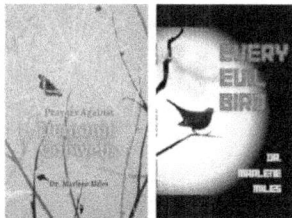

Every Evil Bird https://a.co/d/hF1kh1O

Every Evil Arrow
https://a.co/d/afgRkiA

Gates of Thanksgiving

Spirits of Death & the Grave, Pass Over
Me and My House
https://a.co/d/dS4ewyr

*Please note that my name is spelled
incorrectly on amazon, but not on the book.*

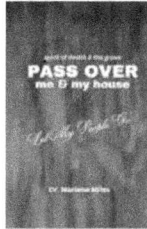

Throne of Grace: Courtroom Prayer

https://a.co/d/fNMxcM9

Warfare Prayer Against Poverty
https://a.co/d/bZ61lYu

www.ingramcontent.com/pod-product-compliance
Lightning Source LLC
LaVergne TN
LVHW021357080426
835508LV00020B/2317